F*CK CANCER

Losing My Mom:
Real, Raw, Unapologetic Grief

F*CK CANCER

Losing My Mom:
Real, Raw, Unapologetic Grief

K. DANIELLE

RED INK
PUBLISHING

Copyright © December 2020 by Red Ink Publishing. All rights reserved.

Editor: Jessica Youmans, Willkie Nine Publishing and Editorial Services

Red Ink Publishing, PO Box 531814, Indianapolis, IN 46253

FIRST EDITION

ISBN (paperback): 978-1-7355235-0-7
ISBN (ebook): 978-1-7355235-1-4

Library of Congress Cataloging-in-Publication Data
Name: Danielle, K., author
Title: Fuck Cancer Losing My Mom: Real, Raw, Unapologetic Grief/K. Danielle
Identifiers:
Library of Congress Control Number: 2020914530

Printed in the United States of America.

CONTENTS

In

Loving Memory

of

Zerlin Dean Jones

07/14/1963-10/19/2017

PREFACE

F*ck cancer! Yes, I said it. Over the past few years, I've probably said it at least a thousand times. Maybe more. But it's how I feel. It's how I've felt since I first heard "your mom" and "cancer" in the same sentence.

If I have to be honest, I didn't want to write this book. In fact, I have avoided it like the plague ever since it was dropped in my spirit nearly three years ago. It was a few months before my life changed forever. I'll never forget that day. God gave me a vision of the cover of this book, although the title was different. One minute I was cleaning the granite countertop, preparing to cook breakfast, and the next minute I was sobbing on the kitchen floor. With eyes full of tears, I sent my friends a message in our group chat. I needed them to know what God had said, just in case I tried to push it aside later.

I was supposed to start writing this book the day after I buried my mother. Instead, I decided that just like my mother's death, the vision of that book was all a bad dream that, unfortunately, I couldn't escape.

And then, the calling happened again. Shortly before enduring the second Christmas holiday without my mother, I felt God telling me to do a series of videos about grief. These would require that I be completely transparent about my battle with grief. It would require that I faced the pain of the loss of my mother head-on. It would require that I stopped pretending that it didn't happen.

Although I was terrified, I sat in front of my computer, logged into Facebook, and clicked "Live" every week for four weeks. I didn't know what kind of response I would get, and honestly, it didn't matter. I was obedient to the calling this time. And to my surprise, the response was overwhelming. I received so many encouraging comments and messages. In some small way, I was helping others just by being myself and telling my story. I was raw and I was real. It was what I needed. Feeling this small piece of healing made me wonder if others required that as well. I knew then that I had to write this book.

I am not an expert on grief. I am a daughter trying to learn how to navigate life without her mother. But I know I am not alone. I joined many others trying to navigate life without their mothers. I wrote this book with you in mind. I wrote this book because someone, somewhere needs to hear my story -- my mom's story. I wrote this book because someone, somewhere needs to know it's okay not to be okay. I wrote this book because, quite frankly, I needed to grieve. I am still grieving today. And perhaps someone, somewhere, needs to grieve, too. This book is for you.

"To describe my mother
would be to write about
a hurricane in its perfect
power. Or climbing,
falling colors of a rainbow."

The Late Dr. Maya Angelou

INTRODUCTION

If I tried to paint a picture with words of the phenomenal woman my mom was, I'd fail miserably. Because Zerlin Dean Jones was indescribable.

My mom was a remarkable woman with a huge heart and a zest for life. She loved her family. She loved her friends. She loved her church. She played by her own rules and was unapologetic about it. My mom wasn't perfect and life wasn't always easy.

Mom endured many hardships long before she was diagnosed with cancer. Yet, she proved over and over again that her circumstances didn't define her. She endured heartbreak and an abusive marriage, but she never stopped believing in love. She dealt with issues in her career as a security officer, but maintained a reputation as a dedicated and committed employee with the Louisiana State Penitentiary for almost 20 years. She dealt with insecurities with her weight, but you would never know it because her confidence entered the room before she did.

As with any mother/daughter relationship, we had our moments. When I was younger, I didn't feel like my mom and I were close. There were times that I felt like we were always at each other's throats. As sensitive as my mom could be sometimes, she became a natural at tough love. From about age nine to about age thirteen, our relationship was extremely rocky. I held on to so much resentment for so many things. One day we had an intense argument and I finally told her how I felt. We realized then that the whole time I wanted better for her, she was sacrificing because she wanted better for me. That one conversation changed our relationship forever.

My mom was a single mother and raised me with the help of my grandparents. There was nothing I could ask for that she wouldn't do whatever she could to get it for me or to make it happen for me. I realized the sacrifice that my mom was making for me, so I did whatever I could to make raising me as stress free as possible -- at least when it came to finances anyway. I'm not going to lie. I was a teenager and before the lightbulb clicked, I gave her hell.

I remember one time my mom heard me talking to one of my cousins about some Jordans. I was a tomboy back then and I loved all sneakers, especially Jordans. I knew how much they cost at the time and knew better than to expect my mom, a single mother, to put out that kind of money for some shoes. She asked me if I wanted them. I lied and said no. Needless to say, she didn't believe me. When report cards were sent home the next time after that conversation, you want to know what my reward was for getting six A's and one B? You guessed it. Jordans. That was my mom.

When I told my mom that I wanted to move to Indianapolis after graduation, she was so supportive. Although I was her only child and moving meant that I would be twelve hours away from her, she wanted whatever I wanted as long as I would be happy. At the time, I didn't realistically take into account what that meant. After all, I didn't think I would be here long.

Nonetheless, my mom was present for every major event in my life. She was there for the birth of her first grandchild -- in the room and holding my hand. When I knew my first marriage was over, I called my mom and told her that I needed to get out. I needed to get on my feet and start a new life for me and Kyndal. Without hesitation, she told me to send Kyndal to Mississippi so that I could do just that. It was one of the hardest decisions I ever had to make, to be away from my first child. For the first two years of Kyndal's life, my mom raised her. But my heart was at ease because I knew without a shadow of a doubt that I was making the right decision. And I knew in my heart that my baby would be well taken care of. My mom called me all the time to tell me what Kyndal was up to and she sent me pictures in the mail almost every other week. That was my mom.

She was there when I married my soulmate, and she was there for the birth of both her other grandchildren. She was there when I received my first college degree and she would have been there for my second one if I hadn't discouraged her from trying to travel to the midwest in December. That was my mom.

I could go on and on sharing memories and stories about what made my mom such an amazing woman and why my life was forever changed by her passing. The memories are what keep me going. I wanted you to get a glimpse of the woman with whom I shared thirty-six years of unconditional love with before the disease stole her away from the ones she loved and whom loved her.

As you read this book, I hope you can learn something new about your mom or about yourself that will help you better cope with the tremendous loss. I pray that you gain a clearer perspective on the grieving process and how to better navigate your new normal. I hope that our story moves you and inspires you to continue the legacy of your mom. I pray that it gives you unshakable faith and a hope that you can and will live again.

CHAPTER 1

The Diagnosis

Health Concerns

It was June of 2015. After several trips to Mississippi to visit my mom, I knew I had to have a serious conversation with her about her health. Observations of her on those visits indicated some concerning problems: She generally did not look healthy in any aspect, and I knew her weight was a major contributing factor.

My mom had issues with her weight my entire life. But something was different this time. I didn't know what it was but I didn't like what I saw. I was nervous about talking to my mom. Her weight was a sensitive issue as it always had been. I'm so glad that I didn't let that nervousness prevent me from having the conversation.

I was surprised when my mom shared similar concerns as we talked, and within three weeks, she applied for a leave of absence from her employer to begin her journey back to health at home with me in Indianapolis.

For the first time in a long time, I saw excitement in my mom's eyes. We started making all kinds of plans to travel and do things together. I was excited to spend time with her for a few months. It would be the first time in fifteen years that we would be under the same roof, even if it was for a short period of time.

I didn't understand the magnitude or how valuable this time was until months later.

Weight Loss Journey

I contacted my friend Eve Guzman, Nutrition Specialist and owner of G-Transformation Academy, for a meal plan and workout guide for my mom. Her weight loss journey was underway, but there was a lot of work to do.

It wasn't all work, though. My mom and I had so much fun during this time. It was the first time since high school that I was able to spend every single day with her. We cooked together, worked out together, laughed together, and watched our favorite shows together. Every. Single. Day. She got to spend those months loving on her grandchildren. She enjoyed having her son-in-love spoil her, making her favorites like spaghetti and steak (not at the same time, of course). It was some of the best times of our lives. I thank God for them.

Between July 2015 and September 2015, my mom lost a total of 42 pounds. I was so proud of her and she was equally proud of herself. After this success, she returned to Mississippi. She was so excited to continue her journey. She checked in with me regularly to let me know her progress. I helped her plan her meals, and she was faithful to her weekly weigh-ins. We were planning a photoshoot for her when she hit her fifty pound milestone. I was already shopping for her new wardrobe.

Those weren't the only plans we had. We had plans to see the world. My mom had never flown before. Never! Although she had a fear of flying, it was primarily because of her weight that she had never flown. With this new determination to lose weight, we started to make plans to travel. Our first stop was going to be Las Vegas, her choice. We had it all mapped out. On her 53rd birthday, we would be in Vegas! But my mom noticed something strange. Although she was losing weight, her right leg was noticeably larger than her left. Her first thought was that she was retaining fluid, so she scheduled an appointment with her primary care physician. Her doctor ordered some tests. I still haven't made it to Vegas yet.

Devastating News

A few short weeks later, in November 2015, we received the devastating news. I had just arrived home from work. I was in the middle of clicking the button on the garage door opener when my phone rang. It was my Aunt Wyntress (I miss her so much! She passed away just seven months after my mom). I was so happy to hear from her. I thought it would be a call to tell me that my mom had fluid on her knee and that she needed to rest it, elevate it, and take some over-the-counter pain medicine. That she was going to be as good as new. But that's not what my aunt said. She didn't say that because it wasn't fluid. She said the "c" word instead.

I don't know how long my aunt had been calling my name before I responded. I just remember her asking me where I was and if I was okay. Thank God I was sitting in my driveway. The diagnosis was Stage II Sarcoma Cancer. The tumor was located in her right thigh and measured 18.1 x 9.3 x 11.4 cm. The rest of the conversation was me asking her a barrage of questions, one of which was, "What the hell is a sarcoma?" This type of tumor, leiomyosarcoma, is one of the thirteen common types of soft tissue sarcomas. I wrote down every word she said and went over it several times. I needed to know what this was and how we were going to get rid of it.

The sound of my mom's voice on the phone broke my heart, yet gave me peace at the same time. I knew I needed to be there. It broke my heart that I wasn't there with her when she heard the news. I could tell she was afraid, even though at the time she didn't admit it. But I knew my mom was strong. I knew she was ready for the fight of her life.

I ended the call, and the tears began to fall free and fast. I whispered to no one but myself and God, "My mom has can..." I couldn't even finish the word. Before I knew it, I was yelling and screaming. I couldn't breathe. It was the first panic attack I'd had in months. This could not be happening!

I finally got myself together and dragged myself into the house. I had barely put my work bag and keys down when I grabbed my laptop and sat down at the kitchen table. I needed to know all there was to know about this disease, so I would know what we were up against. I needed to know what questions to ask. I needed to know our options for treatment. I needed to know that there was a cure for us. I was determined that my mom was not going to fight this alone. That wasn't HER diagnosis. That was OUR diagnosis.

At the time of diagnosis, I was working on my first book. It was a collection of poetry I had written over ten years. It was finally happening. My dream of becoming a published author was right around the corner. My mom couldn't have been more proud. She was always my biggest cheerleader (my husband, too) when it came to my writing. Reading and writing was a love we both shared.

I don't know how many times we talked about me pursuing writing full-time one day. It usually ended with her telling me to hurry up so she could retire early. My mom's dreams for me were so big. They were New York Times BestSeller big! (Yikes!) She would tell me all the time. And I know she believed in her dreams for me, even if I didn't.

A few days after her diagnosis, she asked me for an update on my book. What book? *Woman, I'm not thinking about a book right now.* I told her that I wasn't worried about that right now. Without missing a beat, she said, "And why not?" I didn't get to answer the question. Apparently, it was rhetorical because she went on to tell me how I was going to finish the book and get it published. End of discussion.

Three days before Christmas, my book, "Pieces of My Reflection," was published. Two days after Christmas, I boarded a flight from Indianapolis to Baton Rouge, LA, to be with my mom as she started chemotherapy. We were both afraid of the unknowns. There just wasn't enough information about the treatment of this rare cancer to ease our minds. According to the Cancer Treatment Centers of America website, "Leiomysarcomas are uncommon, malignant tumors that grow from immature smooth muscle cells and account for 10-20 percent of all soft tissue sarcomas." The information didn't tell us anything. We were afraid of the side effects of chemotherapy and we were worried it wouldn't work. We were just scared.

CHAPTER 2

The Battle

My mom's battle with this terrible disease lasted about a year and eleven months. During this time, she was in and out of the hospital. It progressed so fast. She literally went from working out and losing weight to being almost immobile in a matter of months. One treatment after the other, the doctors tried to get it under control. At every turn, we were met with adversity. We were fighting an uphill battle.

Chemotherapy

The side effects of the chemotherapy started off minimal. My mom and I were relieved that she was blessed enough not to experience the worst of the side effects, though doctors prepared us for the worst. We had watched enough movies with "c" patients to have an idea of what to expect. Thank God she didn't have to experience all that we saw in those stories.

There were two rounds of chemotherapy. The first round was a stay in the hospital. I can admit that I was so afraid that I didn't sleep at night during that time. My mom barely slept herself but that was primarily because the nurses were in her room what felt like around the clock. As soon as she would doze off, they would need to come in to give meds or check vitals. They were always in and out, especially when I had to summon them to help my mom to the bathroom. My mom and I had this running joke because every time she had to go to the bathroom, so did I. We needed something to make us laugh.

I remember one night when my mom woke up and I was awake, flipping through the channels. It had to be about four o'clock in the morning. She gave me her mom-look. "Danielle," she said in her mom-voice. She often called me by my middle name when I was in trouble. I chuckled.

"Yes, mom?"

"Why are you up?" she asked.

"I was just waiting for you to have to go to the bathroom." I laughed.

She did have to go, too -- right before she told me to turn off the TV and get some rest.

We tried to make the best of the time we spent together. We watched my mom's favorite judge shows and the only movies we watched were comedies. My mom loved to laugh. Her laugh was infectious. And as the cliché goes, it was good for her soul. Mine, too.

After several weeks of chemotherapy, both in the hospital and as an outpatient, we learned that it was ineffective and that it was hurting her condition. The combination of the two drugs initially given caused swelling, further limiting her mobility. The oral chemotherapy didn't work either. It caused hair loss, and while the swelling was reduced, the drugs were not strong enough to slow the growth of the cells.

Radiation Therapy

The next phase of treatment was radiation, so for six (or eight) weeks, my mom underwent radiation therapy. This course of treatment was focused on the primary tumor in her thigh, with the hope of slowing the growth or killing the tumor, while protecting her other organs. If radiation therapy was successful, the focus would then shift to the small cells that were now growing on her lungs. (Unbeknownst to me at this time, cancer had already metastasized to her lungs.)

This treatment was going to work. This treatment had to work.

As I told you in the last chapter, my first book was published days before my mom started chemotherapy. I wanted to put the book on hold, but my mom (and my husband) wouldn't let me. So I continued with the launch as planned. Well, sort of. By this time, my mom was almost entirely immobile, and travel was out of the question. This meant that my mom was not going to be at my first book signing. This was her dream, too, and I was devastated that she wasn't going to be there.

One night I was talking to my husband about the book signing and how heartbroken I was that my mom couldn't be there, and I shared how I wanted to cancel the event altogether.

"Have the book signing at home." The words came out of his mouth so smoothly, as if he was thinking it all along. I'm not sure why I didn't think of that, but it didn't matter. I was grateful that he did. I started planning the next day. Over a week's time, I booked a venue, hired a photographer, and created the event on Facebook, inviting as many family and friends that I could. I was excited again. About the book. About the event. About the fact that my mom would be there. That was all that mattered.

The event was terrific. It was all that I thought it would be. Yes, I was a ball of nerves. But all I had to do was look on the front row to my right. There she was with her JustasPoetic (my pseudonym) t-shirt, and a hat, sitting in her wheelchair, smiling from ear to ear.

When the event was over, I opened it up to the audience to ask questions or give some words of encouragement. It was so much fun. I was surrounded by so many of my family, classmates -- even my elementary school principal,

Ms. McGhee, was there! I was asked about my writing journey and about some of the poems I read. And then my mom asked to speak. She did what I knew she would do. There wasn't a dry eye in the room. And yes, she ruined my make-up.

My mom had her final radiation treatment about a week later. I'll never forget that day. I made a ridiculously bright sign documenting the day, which included the hashtag #ZStrong, thanks to my Aunt Tammie. I still have the video of her ringing the bell. From time to time, I watch the video and cry. I still miss her so much.

Much to our dismay, radiation therapy was not successful. My mom's medical team refocused their efforts on the cancer cells developing in her lungs until they could create a new plan to attack the tumor in her thigh.

May 25, 2016 (unedited)

It was only two days ago that I sat in an office, with the support of my cousin, Michael, across from the man in the white lab coat. His uneasiness about my visit didn't help the uneasiness I already felt. But I needed answers that only he could provide. I needed him to explain my Mama's most recent CT scan results. He wasn't sure what he could tell me, which is why he immediately asked to confirm with my mama that he could talk to me. I picked up the phone and called her so that she could tell him that it was okay. That worried me. And the next words out of his mouth confirmed that fear.

My heart sank as the man in the white lab coat, Dr. Shows was his name, told me that the cancer had metastasized to my mama's lungs. Stage 4. I sat there, trying to catch my breath as he went on to tell me that he "couldn't cure my mother" and that this course of treatment she had begun was merely to control the spread of the cancer cells and prolong her life as long as possible.

My head understood him completely when he explained to me that Mama wouldn't be alive in 5 years. "How long?" The words slipped from my mouth like a whisper. I'm not sure I intended to ask the question out loud. But he answered. With treatment, provided that this new set of drugs could control the cancer, she could live anywhere from 6 months to a year. And without treatment, 2-3 months. At that moment, I almost regretted asking the question. Almost.

But my heart, well it's still trying to comprehend this new prognosis. After all, these last CT scan results were supposed to show that the tumor was decreasing in size and it was time to have it removed. Those results were supposed to show that Mama's test was over and her testimony was soon to follow. Instead, those results showed that she was dying.

Question after question, it became harder to breathe and well, the tears began to flow. My cousin picked up where I left off, asking the other questions I intended to, but couldn't until there were no more questions left to ask.

He was so compassionate and honest as he expressed to us how he really hoped he would have better news, but at this point, my mama would need a miracle. My cousin and I thanked him for the information as we exited his office in silence. We sat in his car, again in silence, until he reached out his hand. I placed my hand in his and he began to pray out loud, as I prayed silently. We prayed for a miracle.

Radio Frequency Ablation

After the completion of radiation therapy, Mom's surgical oncologist presented us with another treatment option for the primary tumor. It was extremely risky and there was no guarantee of success. I knew my mom was a fighter and it did not surprise me that she wanted to keep trying to beat this disease. The new treatment was called radio frequency ablation, or RFA, an attempt to burn the tumor from the inside.

Heartbreakingly for us, it was yet another unsuccessful treatment, which resulted in an open wound that took a tremendous amount of assistance and guidance in the healing process from the wound care specialists. As I recall the conversation that my mom and I had about the ablation treatment, I remember seeing the defeat in her eyes. I remember hearing the weariness in her voice. She was tired of fighting but she wasn't giving up, even though she was tired. She still had faith that God would see her through. Sadly, though, by September 2017, a little over a month before my mom's passing, she was completely immobile.

June 26, 2016 (unedited)

It's been 33 days since I last talked about my meeting with Dr. Shows. It doesn't mean that I haven't thought about that day ever since. It doesn't mean that sometimes, out of nowhere, his voice, his words, don't cut into me like a double-edged sword. It means that I wish I never had to sit across from him in the first place. Those are the days in which this whole ordeal is the hardest. I constantly remind myself that none of that matters. He is a man, a well-educated man in the field of oncology who answered my questions and provided his expert opinion based on the information, test results, and experience that he has with this type of cancer. However, I was raised to believe that God has the final say. It's not just what I was raised to believe, but it is His promises that I must stand on. It is His promises that I must have faith in. It is in His process that I must trust. But sometimes I can't help but wonder what that "final say" looks like. According to Dr. Shows, we need a miracle.

On the days that my thoughts seem to go to a deeply heartbreaking place, I pick up the phone and call my mama. Some days it gives me strength. I can hear her strength through the phone and I smile. She is in good spirits and I'm grateful. Other days it makes me sad. Our conversations are short and I can only assume that she is in pain or having a rough day. It makes me want to get in a car or on a plane and go be with her. And when the reality hits that I can't, well it hurts.

But today, I'm here (Mississippi)! I've been here for the past five days. My kids are with me. And although they are driving me up a wall, it has been a joy to watch them love on their Maw Maw. They love her so much. Throughout the day, they hardly leave her room. They just want to be around her and I know that she is enjoying every minute of it, especially playing some of her favorite games like Candy Crush and the million cooking games she downloaded on her phone and tablet. It's the little things that mean so much, like my husband driving down for the weekend to see her and grill a steak for her, *since she loved his steak and his spaghetti. The little things. Like me taking the time to shave her head. The little things.*

    This experience, this test, it's scary. And when I think about how this must make my mom feel, well, my heart aches. But I can't help but feel grateful, too: For every second -- of every minute, of every hour, of every day, of every month. I'm grateful for every moment He has given me with my mama and for whatever time we have left. I just want every day to be filled with the love and the joy that she has given me since the day I was born.

CHAPTER 3

The End

The Beginning of the End

I can't remember what I was doing when my NaNa called me to ask if I had heard from my mom. She had tried to call her cell phone several times, but no one answered. I told her that I would try. And I did. No answer. To my surprise, I didn't become alarmed at first. There were several reasons to justify the unanswered calls. My mom was probably asleep. Or maybe the nurses were helping her to the restroom. Or she didn't hear her phone. I can remember not feeling worried at all. I had no reason to. Yes, she was in yet another facility. But she was doing okay. It had been a year and four months since Dr. Shows told me that my mom was dying. She was still here, and she was still fighting.

It wasn't until I got a text from my mom that I started to worry a little. She told me to call my NaNa and let her know she was okay, but that she couldn't talk on the phone. I didn't understand why. I was just about to respond when my phone rang.

It was a nurse from the facility. My mom couldn't talk on the phone because they had to put her on oxygen. She needed help breathing. Her lungs were filling up with fluid.

"I think you need to get here."

Those were the next words out of the nurse's mouth. Within thirty minutes, I booked a flight, packed a bag, and called my Aunt Tammie to tell her that something was wrong and I needed to go see my mom. About an hour later, I was boarding American Airlines flight 1129, headed to Louisiana. Several hours later, I walked into my mom's hospital room and saw the oxygen mask on her face. Another crack in my already broken heart. I really tried to be strong. The pep talks that I had given myself on the plane, as I waited on the connecting flight, on the other plane, in the rental car, were a complete waste of time. It was the first time during her battle with this vicious disease that I cried in front of her. I held her hand, and we sat in silence and tears.

"I don't want to leave you."

She squeezed my hand to get my attention. I'm not sure where my mind was that I didn't notice she was trying to talk to me. Though the humming of the oxygen machine and the mask muffled her voice, I heard her as plain as day. "I don't want to leave you."

No More Treatment Options

For several days, they drained fluid from my mom's lungs. There was so much fluid. Her lungs were so compromised that she had to be monitored in ICU.

She was alert. She was talking. She was eating, but she was dying.

Sometime between when I arrived days earlier to find my mom with the oxygen mask on her face, to sitting in the small, cold conference room with my family, God gave me strength. Even if it was fleeting, it was strength nonetheless.

"I'm sorry, but there's nothing else we can do."

My family and I sat and listened while my mom's medical team told us that all treatment options had been exhausted and what our next steps were. My Aunt Tammie asked some questions. I thanked the doctors for caring for my mom. I don't remember anything else about the small, cold conference room.

All I could hear in my head as we all stepped into the hallway was, "There's nothing else we can do." The words played over and over as I watched my family take in the news, hug, and cry. And as I watched, I made a decision that I didn't have time to process it all. I needed to get myself together to be there for my mom and make the decisions I needed to make for as long as I had left to make them. I needed to be able to make the phone calls to extended family members and friends. I needed to be able to prepare them to say goodbye.

I asked Dr. Lyons if I could be the one to tell my mom the news. I needed to be the one to do it. I didn't want the medical jargon, the business-like tone that lacked compassion (not on purpose because they are just doing their job). It had to be me.

I remember that day so vividly. It was October 5, 2017. I had called the family and friends that I wanted to come to see her. I was selective. She needed a lot of love and a lot of laughter. Our family and friends delivered. We had so much fun that day. We occupied two hospital rooms, and for hours, she was surrounded by people who loved her.

When the crowd began to dwindle, I asked the remaining family members to step out and give my mom and I some privacy. At first, we just held hands and sat in silence, taking in the moment. I could feel that she knew I didn't have good news. And I was right because as I opened my mouth to speak, she asked me, "Is it bad?"

I fought back the tears as I gently told her that they would have to remove the tubes from her lungs and that they would not be able to drain them again. I told her that the doctors felt they had tried everything they could. I held her hand and told her that she would be transferred to another facility. She asked me, "How long?" All I could say was, "Until…"

The next moments are forever in my mind. We had our last secret conversation, and there was nothing left unsaid. When I think about it, our relationship from the time I was born until that moment told the story of our love. She knew how I felt about her, and she made sure that I knew how she felt about me. She gave me what she knew I would need when she was gone. With family and friends in the next room, we said our goodbyes.

"God has the final say."

That's how she ended the conversation. I let her words linger. I didn't want anything to interfere with it getting from her mouth to God's ears. I don't know how long we sat in the silence of that moment before my mom told me that I could tell the family to come back in the room. But I didn't want to.

"Just a few more minutes, Mama."

> Come to me, all you who are weary and
> burdened, and I will give you rest.
> Matthew 11:28 (NIV)

The next few days were filled with phone call after phone call, decision after decision as I planned to have my mom transferred to a hospice facility. She would need around the clock care that we just couldn't provide at home. I visited the facility that was available the soonest and approved the transfer. Within 24 hours, my mom arrived at Clarity Hospice of Baton Rouge.

Seven Days

My mom was the ONLY patient at the hospital who was alert, talking, and eating a regular diet. She didn't belong there and she wasn't supposed to be there. I don't mean it as an insult to the other patients. I say that to point out that none of this made sense. They gave her a week. Seven days. And here my mom was eating, laughing, talking, joking, watching TV, enjoying her visitors. It was like a party in her room. (Don't worry, we were respectful of the other patients and their families.) But still, this wasn't making sense.

On the eighth day, the representative who helped arrange the transfer asked if she could see me for a few minutes. My mom was asleep so I slipped out of the room to talk to her. There were no conference rooms available so we met in the chapel. She asked me about my mom and if I was satisfied with the care she was receiving, and I was.

But then the conversation took a turn. In summary, the manager wanted to move my mom to another facility.

"Why?" You bet that was the next question out of my mouth, as I shifted my position and looked around to remind myself that I was in church, so to speak. To put it gently, as she tried to do, Clarity was a short-term hospice facility, and due to my mom's condition, they expected that she would have passed away within a few days.

She apologized as she felt that it seemed insensitive (You're damn right, it was insensitive!), and she hated to be the one to have to tell me. I must admit I was furious. But I was not about to act a fool and jeopardize my mom's health, especially not knowing how much time we had left.

I politely told her that I understood and that she didn't have to apologize for doing her job. But I made it abundantly clear that my mom would not be moved to another facility. I requested a meeting with whoever was in charge as soon as possible. The bottom line was that no one knew how many days my mom had left and I wasn't about to let anyone further compromise her life. After the meetings, my mom was not transferred.

She Knew, And She Was Ready

The next few days were a blur. The nurses were in and out of the room, my mom was in and out of sleep, and I was in and out of reality.

I didn't sleep at night. I stayed awake most of the time watching her breathe. I only felt comfortable napping during the day because that was when the nurses came to the room more frequently. This was my routine anytime I was with her in any facility or hospital. I didn't sleep at night then. I don't sleep at night now.

I remember when the doctor came in to check her breathing. I could tell by the look on his face when he removed the stethoscope that it wasn't right. My mom did, too, and she quickly said to him that she didn't want to know. He was about to insist on it until he saw my face. I motioned for him to step outside, and I followed. I didn't want to know either, but yet, I had to know. Her breathing was becoming more labored and faint.

"I don't want to know."

The kids were on spring break and were at my NaNa's house, about an hour away. She wanted me to go get them so she could see them. But not before I braided her hair. I asked her if she needed anything before I left since I would be gone for a few hours, and she said no. As I was leaving, she asked me, "Do I look sick?" Her question caught me entirely by surprise. She had never asked that before.

"No," I said because my mom didn't look sick. She looked like my mom. She seemed to be satisfied with my answer. I was going to be bringing the kids back with me. She didn't want to look like she was sick. The kids and my grandmother stayed for several hours before I had to take them back home. They talked, laughed, watched TV, and played games with her on her tablet, all while she held conversations off and on with NaNa. They even had lunch with her. She was saying goodbye to her grandkids and her mom.

When it was time to go, my oldest daughter, Kyndal, stayed behind while I took my grandmother and younger kids to the truck. About 10 minutes later Kyndal got in the truck. I asked her what took so long and she just said she was, "Talking to her Maw Maw." (I would later find out that Kyndal was recording a video that my husband had requested.) I drove them back home and then headed back to the hospice facility to spend what ended up being my last night with my mom.

I tried to stay awake that night but I was so exhausted. I slept. For the first time in a long time, I slept.

My Life Changed Forever

When I woke up that morning, I had no idea that it would be my mom's last day on this earth. Yes, the doctors told me that there was nothing else they could do. Yes, we were currently in a hospice facility, but losing my mom that day was far from any reality I could expect.

Bear with me as this will be the hardest part of the book to write.

I remember EVERYTHING about that day. I needed to take care of some things for my mom that morning, but I was sound asleep. I didn't hear my mom calling my name. To get my attention, she threw ice cubes at me. Four to be exact. I laugh when I think about that. There were no indications that today was the day. There were no signs. Nothing. We laughed about the ice cubes, I got dressed, and then I got my marching orders about what I needed to take care of for her.

While I was waiting to get my mom's truck, I tried to get as much work done as possible. I wanted to spend the rest of the day with my mom with no distractions. I knew that my time with her was coming to an end. I felt it. But I wasn't worried about that happening on that day.

We had lunch, talked, and laughed while watching her judge shows. We both had a kid's meal from Raising Cane's, a restaurant in the south famously known for its chicken tenders. Judge Mathis had just gone off. The cell service in her room was horrible so I told my mom I was going to step outside and make a few quick calls. I had to return a call for work, check on the kids who were at my NaNa's house, and let family and friends know how she was doing. I kissed my mom on the forehead and told her I loved her. I was only going outside, but this was routine anytime I left her presence, whether for a few days or a few minutes.

Ten minutes. Ten minutes later and my life changed forever. My phone rang and it was a staff member from the hospice facility. She asked me where I was and I told her I was sitting outside. She asked me if I could come back in now. I heard the urgency in her voice. And when she met me at the entrance door, I saw the panic in her face. All she had the opportunity to say was, "It's your mom."

I rushed into the room and the rest was a nightmare. The nurses tried to explain to me what was happening but I couldn't comprehend them over my screams begging God not take my mom. *Bargaining.*

I was hysterical. I couldn't breathe and I watched as my mom couldn't breathe either. She was leaving me. One of the nurses came over and held me and asked me if there was someone I could call. I don't know how I was able to focus enough to call my husband, but I did. When he answered, all he heard was me sobbing on the phone, trying to tell him that my mom was leaving me.

"She's leaving me, baby!"

The nurse rubbed my head as I held my mom's hand. I asked the nurse if my mom could still hear me. "Yes," she said. Knowing that she could still hear me changed something within me. My heart was breaking by the second but I didn't want the last thing my mom heard was her daughter screaming in agony. With about as much strength as I could muster, I told my mom how much I loved her and how much I would miss her. And even though it was a lie, I told her I would be ok.

I wasn't okay then. I'm not okay now.

My mom took her last breath. My heart, my best friend, my biggest supporter was gone. For the rest of that day, I was tasked with having to break the news to family and my mom's friends. There was no time to process anything that I had just endured. As some of the family arrived at the facility to see my mom and support me, I buried all of my emotions so I could be there for them and comfort them. *I need to be strong* is what I told myself.

I deceived myself. I didn't need to be strong. My family and my friends weren't requiring me to be strong. I put that on myself. If anything, I was allowed to be angry, to scream, or ball up in the fetal position and weep. I was allowed to do it all. But I chose to be strong because I had convinced myself that it was my only option.

In hindsight, I would have made that decision a hundred times over again. It was what prepared me for the coming days. My mom was gone and I had a funeral to plan.

I needed strength.

My Last Goodbye

Saying goodbye to my mom was the hardest thing I've ever done. The dreams were no longer just dreams. I shouldn't call them dreams -- they were nightmares. Nonetheless, it was happening. I had a funeral to plan.

Even though I was my mom's only child, with the love and support I received from family and friends, I never felt alone. They were with me every step of the way. I wasn't alone when I picked out her casket. Or when I chose what she was going to wear. I wasn't alone when I chose the pictures for her obituary. Or when I decided who would be a part of her homegoing service.

The evening before her funeral, I scheduled a viewing. I wanted to make sure that her co-workers who loved her dearly, and anyone who may have had to work on the day of her funeral (her funeral was held on a Friday) would have the opportunity to pay their respects. My mom was so loved, and although I knew I would not be able to accommodate everyone, I had to try, for her.

I wasn't supposed to stay. I was only supposed to greet a few people for the first thirty minutes or so and then leave. That was it. I told myself that I could do that. But when we pulled up to the church and I saw the hearse, that all changed. Suddenly, I couldn't wrap my mind around stepping inside that church to watch as people who loved my mom mourned her. I just wanted to go back to my grandmother's house, curl up in a ball, and cry until I had no tears left. Instead, I sat in silence, staring at the long black car. My husband held my hand until I was ready to go in.

I didn't leave after thirty minutes. I couldn't. I greeted the people who walked through the door and watched as, one by one, sometimes a few at a time, classmates, co-workers, friends, and relatives stood in front of her casket and said their goodbyes. There was something in knowing that my mom touched so many lives that gave me the strength to stay.

I remember waking up the morning of her funeral. I remember getting myself dressed and then checking on my family and keeping myself busy. I was nervous and nauseous and a complete mess on the inside. But I didn't need anyone to see that. I needed to be strong. I knew all eyes were on me. I needed them to know I was okay.

And then it started to hit me. I walked outside to get some fresh air. The emotions were hitting all at once and I needed to breathe. I wasn't outside but a few minutes when the black limousine drove up into the driveway. I couldn't breathe. If my Uncle Mike had not been standing there, I probably would've passed out. My husband, our three kids, and my grandmother got into the limo while the rest of the family got in their respective cars for the ten minute drive to the church. It really only takes about five minutes, but as you know, funeral processions are slow. It felt like forever.

About fifteen minutes before the service started, my husband, myself, and our kids walked to the front of the church to say our final goodbyes to my mom. It was like an out-of-body experience. I watched as our children looked upon their Maw Maw, as they affectionately called her, one last time. My husband escorted them out as my god-sister, and my best friends stood with me one last time. And as I had done so many times over the previous two years whenever it was time for me to leave her, I kissed her forehead and told her I loved her. One. Last. Time.

And as they closed the casket, I watched as employees from the Louisiana State Penitentiary, where she was employed for almost twenty years, gave her a final salute.

After making it through that moment, I honored my best friend on Friday, October 27, 2017, with a short but spiritual homegoing service at her home church, New Zion Hill Baptist Church in Woodville, MS. Her beloved Pastor, (also her first cousin) Pastor Tyser Brown, Sr., gave the eulogy. As I had done so many times in the dreams I had for several months before her passing, I stood at the front of our church with Saniya, my middle daughter, holding my hand.

"I know that it has to be the strength of God that I can stand here today. I've stood here so many times in the last six months in my dreams. The same recurring dream. Every time, I stood before my family and friends, and all the people who loved and cherished my mother. Every time, I stood to talk about my best friend. The difference is that today, it isn't a dream.

Two years ago, when my mother was diagnosed with sarcoma cancer, I was devastated. I heard the "c" word, and I completely lost it. I cried. I screamed. I asked why, but I also prayed. I prayed harder than I've ever prayed for anything in my life. I needed to get myself together so I could be strong for my Mama. Little did I know, I didn't need to be strong. She was strong enough for both of us.

I've known this woman my whole life, but the strength, the courage, the bravery that my Mama showed during this battle with cancer...indescribable. My cousin, Michael, said it best when he said that my Mama fought this disease with laughter, dignity, and grace, as only she could. And that she did. Even in her sickness, she still cared about you and how you were doing. Ask anyone who ever called to check on her or came to see her. She wanted to know that you were doing okay. But that was just her. I can remember so many conversations that we had, even when she wasn't feeling her best, she needed to know her baby was doing okay. And if I wasn't feeling well, no matter how I tried to cover it up, she knew it. She worried about me more than I worried about her. That was my Mama.

Her strength... There are just no words. Some days I would look at her and I couldn't believe the battle she was fighting. She didn't look like what she was going through. She didn't sound like what she was going through. A fighter! My mom was a fighter. She fought this disease with everything that was in her and then some. Whenever there was a bad report from the doctor, she "put it under her feet."

When I think about our relationship, I can't help but thank God. He couldn't have blessed me with a more perfect mother. He gave me thirty-six years of unconditional love and lots of laughter. Thirty-six years of hugs, kisses, tears, whippings, sacrifice, conversations, and secrets. He gave me thirty-six years of support. My Mama was there for everything important to me. She was there when I married the wrong man (and helped me divorce him, too), and she was there when I married the right one.

She was there for the birth of all three of her grandkids. She was there when I graduated from college with my first degree. She was there to celebrate with us when my husband adopted our eldest daughter, Kyndal. She was my biggest supporter and cheerleader when I published my first book. She even had a chance to see Kyndal play soccer, and a chance to see Saniya and Tre play basketball. For thirty-six years, she was always there.

My Mama lived a remarkable life. One of service, sacrifice, kindness, and gratitude. God gave her fifty-four years to love and be loved. To cherish and be cherished. She was indeed one of a kind. She had a personality out of this world: The life of the party at all the family gatherings. And she had a heart of gold.

If you knew my Mama -- I mean really knew my Mama -- and you were blessed enough to be a part of her life, I hope that you learned something through her journey with this disease. I hope you learned how to have faith in the face of adversity. Because she did. I hope you learned to stand on God's word, no matter what. Because she did. I hope you learned how to be a light in someone else's life, even when it feels like you are in darkness. Because she was. And I hope you learned that laughter can sometimes be the best medicine. Because she definitely taught you that.

To my family, I know that I don't have to thank you for anything that you have ever done for my Mama, especially during this time. I know that you wouldn't have had it any other way. I know how much you loved her, and you definitely know how much she loved each of you. And to my husband, thank you! You made so many sacrifices so that I could take care of my Mama for two years. You never complained. You always told me to do whatever I needed to do and you would take care of the rest. Anyone who ever talked to my Mama, they knew how much she loved her son-in-law. Sometimes I felt like I was the daughter-in-law who married her son. To my babies, know that your Maw Maw loved you with all her heart and was so proud of you. Cherish your memories with her and carry them in your heart.

My Mama has transitioned to her heavenly home. We, too, are transitioning. We are transitioning into the next phase of our lives, without our ray of sunshine. Without our life of the party. But my Mama hasn't left us. She just has a different role. She is our angel now. Free of pain and completely healed. This won't be easy. But when we have those difficult moments, we will let her love, her smile, and her laughter comfort you. Wrap yourself in the memories you have of her and know that she is with God.

I will never forget our last two weeks together. It was the funniest, scariest, and most intimate time I had spent with my mom throughout her journey. Those memories are forever in my heart as I learn how to live in this new season with my Mama -- my best friend, my cheerleader -- my ride or die as my guardian angel.

Rest in God, Mama. I'll always love you and will miss you more than I could ever say."

"Being strong does not
mean you won't have
moments of weakness."

K. Danielle

CHAPTER 4

Life After Loss

January 20, 2018 (unedited)

Yesterday marked three months since my mama passed. Three whole months. Three whole months since my life changed forever. This constant ache in my chest because the woman who gave me life is gone. Mama is gone. I can't call her and talk to her. I can't hear her laugh. I can't hold her hand. I can't do anything. I can't feel anything. Everything is different. Everything I've ever known is different.

I haven't grieved. I mean like truly grieved. At least I don't feel like I have. Mainly because I've convinced myself, or should I say, I make a conscious, daily effort to convince myself that it just didn't happen. Maybe that's why every night I relive her last moments. Every night I see her take her last breath. And then every morning I convince myself that it was a nightmare. It's easier that way. And even though the ache in my chest is a constant reminder, I try to ignore it. It doesn't work.

It's weird. I'll be driving, or listening to music, or working...hell, it doesn't matter what I'm doing, I'm always thinking about her. I always want to call her just to hear her voice. I know I can't call her, but I can still pretend losing her was all just a nightmare. The only time I don't dream is when I've taken a sleep aid. I hate sleep aids. I don't know why, but I do.

I have insomnia now. Well, I've always suffered from insomnia, but since Mama died, it's a lot worse. Right now, it's 3:08 am and I am wide awake. Why? Because I'd rather stay awake than watch my Mama die in my dreams.

I can't even explain what goes on in my head when I'm pretending it didn't happen. It's what I call putting on my grief mask. It's the only way I can function. And I feel like a crazy person. I feel trapped between my alternate reality and real life. Sometimes I find myself staring at nothing, wondering what I was about to say or do. Sometimes I feel like a zombie, like I'm just wandering through life. When I say nothing is the same, NOTHING is the same. I'm not okay. But too many people need me to be okay, which is another reason I had to become good at pretending. Another reason I wear "the mask."

I'm working on finding a therapist. I really think I need one. I know I need a therapist. I can admit that I'm very nervous about it. I'm scared. I'm scared that she will want to medicate me. Maybe I need medication. No, I need my Mama!

This isn't fair! My Mama was supposed to live a long life and leave this world peacefully surrounded by me and her grands and great-grands. Of course, I would still grieve her. Life would still not be the same. But at least it would make sense! My Mama was not supposed to die at 54 from cancer! What am I supposed to do without her? I can't accept this! Everyone thinks I'm this strong person. But in this life, this new life, I'm broken.

I AM BROKEN!

I experienced a lot of death growing up. I think I was five years old when I attended the funeral for my paternal grandfather, although I didn't really know him. I was in junior high when my paternal grandmother died. Over the rest of my childhood and throughout early adulthood, I would attend countless funerals for the siblings of my grandparents, many of them with whom I had close relationships. I was no stranger to death.

But when my grandfather passed away in 2014, I became familiar with grief. He was the man who raised me, the man who walked me down the aisle (both times), my hero and my heart. He was the first person I would watch take his last breath. Life altering.

I remember someone saying something about the stages of grief but I didn't give it much thought. I'm not sure if I researched it or not. And that time, I didn't think I needed to do that. My grandfather died. I was sad and heartbroken. Case closed.

Not this time. This time I needed to know what to expect after losing my best friend. I needed to know how I would feel and what to do about it. I needed help. I needed answers. I needed my mom. But I'd have to settle for the grief cycle model by Swiss psychiatrist, Elizabeth Kubler-Ross, which identified the five stages of grief.

The more I began to study the five stages of grief, the more I realized that my mom went through these stages as she processed her terminal illness. It is my belief that these stages were never intended to describe or reflect on how a person grieves. Instead, these stages are a gauge to identifying your emotions. It is not a linear timeline in grief, but a cycle in no particular order. Grief is an individual journey, and no one journey is the same.

Five Stages of Grief

Denial

Denial is a buffer zone that can linger for days or years. This was the stage I clung to for dear life. It didn't happen. It didn't happen. IT. DID. NOT. HAPPEN. I don't care that the doctors told me that my mom was going to die, or that God told me that she was going to die. As far as I was concerned, it didn't happen.

But it did happen. I remember it vividly. I remember everything about that day except what I was wearing. I remember her throwing ice cubes at me that morning to get me to wake up because I had to take her truck to the dealership for an oil change. I remember seeing one of her classmates (can't remember which one) and calling her so that he could speak with her. (I tuned out their brief conversation.) I remember stopping at Raising Cane's and getting us both a kid's meal. (I was absolutely sick of food by this time.)

I remember us eating lunch and watching a slew of judge shows. Judge Mathis was the last one we watched. I remember watching her doze in and out of sleep. I remember kissing her on her forehead before leaving her room to go outside and make a couple calls. I remember my phone ringing. I remember the lady on the phone asking me where I was and when I told her I was outside, I remember her meeting me at the door. I remember that my mom was dying.

I remember EVERYTHING. But all I wanted to do was forget.

Denial reared its ugly head less than a month after my mom's funeral. I was scheduled to read my new children's book to about 400 adorable kindergartners at Rosa Parks

Kindergarten Academy. I had an amazing time with the kids and I couldn't wait to get back to my truck so I could call and tell my mom all about it. That was my routine. If my mom wasn't working, she was the first one I called after any event or school visit.

I was beaming. I hurried to my truck to load my books. I put the key in the ignition and grabbed my phone from my purse. All I had to do was press and hold the number 3 because of course my mom's number was on speed dial. Her name popped up on the screen, and next to it were the broken heart and angel emojis. My reminders. I still held the phone to my ear as it went straight to voicemail. My mom was gone. I would never be able to call her again. I'm not sure how long I sat in that parking lot and wept. F*ck cancer!

That moment was one of the lowest moments. I found myself in my truck screaming and hollering. I could barely breathe. It was a different kind of pain, almost as bad as the day my mom died. I knew I wasn't going to be able to handle moments like that. So I put my mom's death on a shelf in the darkest corner of my mind and left it there. But I left it on the shelf for too long.

Anger

I'm not sure when I first realized that I had transitioned to this stage of grief. But man was I pissed! In the words of my NaNa, "I was fighting mad." Although there were brief moments of anger throughout my mom's battle with cancer, nothing compared to the level of anger that arose in me after her passing. I wanted so badly for life to go back to the way it was. Back to when my mom was alive and I could pick up the phone and call her. Back to the time before God gave her the cancer.

In hindsight, it was probably a horrible idea to go back to a toxic and dysfunctional work environment so soon (I don't even think it was two weeks) after her passing. But as the cliché goes, "Hindsight is always 20/20." I wanted a distraction. No, I needed a distraction -- anything to keep my mind busy. Anything to keep me from saying over and over in my head, "My mom is dead." I needed a distraction and what I got was pure hell.

When I first transitioned to this stage, my anger was fixated on one being. And I know I'm going to ruffle some feathers when I say this. I know that what I am going to say is downright controversial, especially if you are overly religious, a holy roller, a Bible thumper...you get my drift. But if you haven't noticed by now, I really don't give a damn. I'm going to say it anyway:

I WAS MAD AT GOD! (Don't make that face! I warned you.)

Yes, that's right! I said it! I was mad at God. Sometimes I find myself still mad at God. I know that statement begs the questions, Why? How? Well, since you asked, here goes. I was mad at God because I expected Him to heal my mom. I expected Him to work one of His miracles that I've been preached to about so many times. You know the one where He fed the five thousand with what was clearly not enough fish. Or when He spit in the blind man's eyes and he could see. (By the way, ewww!) Or when he made the lame man stand up and walk. (And while you are at it grab that bed and take it with you.) Or the one where they ran out of wine at the reception so He made some with water (That one is my favorite). Or the one where He healed my mom of cancer and we just got off the phone talking about nothing. Oh wait, not that one. THAT ONE DIDN'T HAPPEN!

I knew my anger was spiraling out of control. One day, I was sitting at my desk in an incredibly toxic work environment. I opened this email and became furious. I remember cursing at God! I don't think I had ever cursed at God before. I mean, not directly at Him anyway. For the sake of this book, I'll give you the PG version. I remember yelling, "You took my Mama but you let these idiots lie to and steal from your people every week! REALLY?" Three months later, I resigned and started looking for a therapist.

Bargaining

From the day I got the call about her diagnosis until moments before her last breath, I begged God to heal her. I knew that her family and friends that loved her were praying for her. And even if my prayer didn't get past the ceiling, I knew my NaNa's prayers alone should have been enough to save her. I was begging God for my mom. She was begging God for her child.

I felt that what I was asking God to do was simple. Just let one of the treatments work. He didn't have to take it all away (although that would have been ideal). We've all been taught that there is a purpose for everything. If God's purpose for the cancer to develop was to shed more light on this rare form, so be it. If it was so that she could be a living witness for someone else, great. All I asked was that ONE of the treatments worked. I pleaded that just one of them worked. And then I pleaded for Him to stop her from taking her last breath. My begging and pleading didn't work. There was no longer a reason to beg. She was gone.

Depression

Depression was not unfamiliar to me. I had been fighting depression long before my mom's diagnosis. It started out as postpartum depression after my son was born. I was ashamed to admit it. And so what did I do? I tried to hide it. I hid it for six years. After six years it wasn't postpartum anymore. It was just plain old depression. When my mom died, I knew I wouldn't just be able to sweep it under the rug like I tried (and failed) to do in the past.

My battles with both depression and grief (I've learned how to separate the two) are much alike. There are days in which I am winning one and not the other. Then there are days that I wave my little white flag and checkout mentally or end up in the closet in the fetal position weeping.

Before this book, only my husband and my closest family and friends knew about my battle with depression.

And only one person knows what I am about to tell the masses.

I wanted to end it all.

Last year (2019) was by far my lowest year. I carried my worsening depression and my battle with grief into this year. I was a zombie trapped in the fog of life without my mom. Then, several months ago, life without my mom became unbearable. The war in my head and the constant pain in my chest were just too much. I knew that my life changed forever the day my mom died. I realized that I had changed forever. The person I was before October 19, 2017 was lowered in that grave and covered in dirt and a beautiful heart-shaped tombstone. I remember writing in my journal:

Kimberly Danielle

9/22/81-10/19/17

That was the reality. That was my new normal. That was too much for me. And I didn't want to do it.

I was sitting on the bathroom counter with eyes full of tears when I finally let the words, "I don't want to be here anymore," slip from my lips in a whisper (because although it was true, I was ashamed to say it aloud). I buried my head in my husband's neck. I wept. I wept because at that moment, it was selfish. I wept because at that moment, it was true.

I went back to therapy.

Acceptance

I'm not there yet. I won't ever be there. And that's okay with me. It can be okay for you, too. I prefer the term acknowledgement instead.

"Acceptance is an illusion.
Acknowledgement is a healthy state."
- Sharon Davis

In the few years since my mom has passed, I have learned to identify where I am in the grief cycle. I think it is vitally important to know where you are in the cycle. I talked about this with my therapist.

I linger mostly between denial and acknowledgement. Denial helps me to function. I remember the first time I told my therapist this. She asked me to explain and I was hesitant. I didn't know how to explain it in a way that made sense. I didn't want to sound like a crazy person. I didn't know how to "do" therapy. This was all new to me. But I knew enough about therapy to know that it was nothing like writing in my journal. My journal was a safe place. When I first started therapy, I wasn't sure if it was a safe place. I just knew that I needed it to be.

My therapist sensed my hesitance but she didn't rush me. I appreciated her for that. I told her about the grief mask. Of course I had to elaborate. So I did. I explained to my therapist that the same strength that I felt I needed to endure my mom's last moments, plan her funeral and bury her, was the same strength I needed to carry the burden of her death. My husband needed his broken wife and my kids needed their shattered mother.

I hid my grief and only felt comfortable expressing it at certain times. When I told my therapist this, of course she asked me, "Why?" "I don't want to get stuck," I said. I believed that if I allowed myself to feel the totality of my mom's death, that I would never recover. At that time, that was not a risk that I was willing to take.

Surviving Loss

The death of your mother is so colossal. It feels like literal heartbreak; like a part of you dies right along with her. There is no roadmap. It is a roller coaster ride of reminiscing, love and laughter, mood swings, spontaneous weeping, and any other emotion you can imagine. Grief is ugly, unpredictable and messy. You don't just mourn your mom, you mourn the person you were when she was alive, too. For me, it's unrealistic to think that I will ever get over the loss of my mom, a woman I have a lifetime of memories with. You don't get over loss. You adjust to it. The loss of your mom's presence becomes the new normal.

I hated my new normal. I didn't want to feel anything. I detached myself from reality. I thought that if I just kept myself busy enough I wouldn't have time to think. I wanted to be so exhausted that I had no choice but to sleep at night.

The last two and a half years consisted of me putting on my grief mask. I didn't talk about my grief to anyone other than my therapist. I was dishonest with my husband, my children, and my friends. The only time I felt comfortable without the mask was on days or holidays in which it was expected for me to be in mourning.

Hiding behind the mask felt like the only way I could function. In one of my counseling sessions, my therapist and I discussed the mask. She expressed her concern about how I was processing my mom's death. The truth is: I was afraid to grieve. I was afraid that if I allowed myself to feel the totality of losing my mom, that I would never recover.

But what I was doing by wearing the mask wasn't helping. I started to neglect myself. I felt sick most of the time. I preferred to be alone more than ever before. I would pretend to go to the bathroom and sit on the floor in the closet and stare at the wall. I would say that I needed to go to the store and just sit in the parking lot and cry. I couldn't pray. I was neglecting myself physically, emotionally, and spiritually.

My negligence was so bad that I almost cancelled our ten-year anniversary celebration. Before my mom passed, I was looking forward to it. I couldn't wait. My husband and I had talked about it in great detail for over a year. Once the cancer spread and my mom was no longer mobile, we were going to plan a celebration in Mississippi so that she could be a part of it. But after her death, it didn't matter whether we celebrated it or not. She wouldn't be there.

After several conversations with my husband, begrudgingly, I agreed not to cancel it, and instead we planned to spend some quality time with each other and a small celebration with family.

On the morning of our anniversary, my husband entered our room with a laptop in hand, wished me a Happy Anniversary and told me to press play. I sat with tear-filled eyes as some of my family from Mississippi and life-long friends sent us messages of love and congratulations in celebration of our anniversary. I sat there and thought this is the most amazing and thoughtful thing that he could've done. And then the last video played.

I began to weep as I stared at the screen. It was my mom. I was staring at my mom as she wished us a happy anniversary. It all made sense. I was overtaken with emotion of both gratefulness and heartbreak as I came to the realization that this was the video that my husband had asked Kyndal to record, the day before my mom passed away.

A Healthy Way to Grieve

In the beginning, I didn't allow myself to be vulnerable. I was still hanging on to the notion that I had to be strong. I can honestly say that now I am surviving the loss of my mom. I think about her in some way every day. There are no easy days, just days that are more tolerable than others. I had this preconceived notion about what this process would look like and I put unrealistic expectations on myself.

In one of my therapy sessions, my therapist and I discussed if there was a healthy way to grieve. I was skeptical. My therapist took the time to explain how coping with grief was an active process and gave me some homework. She gave me some information to take home and I also did some research on my own.

I came to terms with the fact that the grief of my mom will never end and that I need to learn to be patient with myself. No one can tell me how to grieve or how long to grieve. But I can help the people who love me understand what I need and what helps me.

I can be honest and say that I still struggle with the concept of grieving in a healthy way. I have listed a few things that I have implemented that are helping me to cope with the loss of my mom:

Self-Care. I make a conscious effort to set aside time for myself and I have people who keep me accountable in doing so.

Exercise Regularly. I started simple with walking and yoga a couple times a week.

Journal. This allows me to express myself freely and without judgment. It gives me a safe space to release emotions that could otherwise become suppressed. I am learning how to compartmentalize my emotions. I have a journal specifically for writing about my grief.

Talk to Others. I became more open to talking about my loss with those closest to me. I don't share my grief with everyone. I know who I can call and when. I am open and honest about what does and does not help me.

Accept Help and Support. I can admit that this was the hardest thing to do. My husband was a great help in this area.

Plan Ahead for Grief Triggers. I make plans early for days that I know are going to be emotionally difficult. I communicate my emotions and I don't overcommit.

Carry a Keepsake. I still have notes from my mom because they are written in her handwriting, along with countless other keepsakes. My mother-in-love, Cheryl, made some earrings and a necklace from one of my mom's dresses.

What <u>Not</u> to say to Someone who is Grieving?

This section of the book is for those of us who are grieving a loss, and for those of you who have not yet lost someone, to better understand your loved one or friend who is dealing with the life-altering loss of their mother.

For those of us who are grieving, have the confidence to let people know what does and does not help you. This helps us to realize just how much control we have over the people we allow to help us through this difficult time.

For those of you who are reading this book to learn how to help your loved one or your friend, this section is to help you understand your role as a supporter and help you understand how to show empathy and compassion.

Let me be clear. I do not intentionally mean to offend or condemn anyone. My intention is to show you how to be gentle, supportive and considerate by shedding some light on things that should *not* be said to a person who is grieving.

This is my personal list. I shared this list during my video series entitled, "Life Without Her," on Facebook live in December 2018. Some of you may find some of the sayings on this list to be helpful to you. If so, I'm happy that hearing these things bring you comfort. But if you are like me, then I hope this gives you the courage to speak up for yourself and your needs, and helps to enlighten others. These statements are in no particular order.

God needed another soldier in his army, rose in his garden, angel in heaven, blah, blah, blah.

To be absent from the body is to be present with the Lord.

I know how you feel.

She got her wings.

She will always be in your heart.

You will see her again.

If you need me, call me.

We will all die one day. (You don't say! *insert eyeroll*)

God makes no mistakes. (I can't stress this enough. STOP. SAYING. THIS.)

Weeping may endure for a night, but joy comes in the morning.

If you have said any of these statements or similar statements, ask yourself this: Would this make me feel comforted? When a person loses their mother, they've lost the person that gave them life. They've lost their sense of identity. They've lost one of the most important people in their life. The dynamics of their family has changed, forever.

A few of those statements are scriptures. Don't get me wrong. There is nothing wrong with relying on scripture for comfort if that works for you. But when you have suffered a loss as life-altering as that of your mother, stop immediately trying to appeal to the spiritual side of that person. The last thing I wanted to hear after my mom passed was a scripture. My heart was broken. My heart is still broken.

I would offer this advice: If you don't know what to say, error on the side of caution and don't say anything. Stay away from clichés. Grief can make even well-meaning people uncomfortable. It is important to try to do your best to understand what a person might be feeling. Sometimes, just admitting that you don't know what to say, offering your condolences, and praying for the person can be of great comfort.

Here are a few ways to be supportive:

Be an Attentive Listener. Let the person who is grieving lead the conversation. You are the passenger.

If you call them or if they call you, give them your full attention and don't interrupt them. Let them tell stories about their loved one and speak freely. Do not make the conversation about you.

Understand that their moods will change and their emotions will come in waves. Don't take things personally. Understand that they are trying their best.

Be consistent. Check-in often. The cards and calls usually stop after the first couple of weeks following the funeral. If you can be there for the long haul, do so.

Don't Judge Them. This is their new normal. Try to be understanding of the roller coaster ride of emotions. We all process grief differently.

Don't Give Unsolicited Advice. Remove words like, "should" from your vocabulary. Trust me, you have no idea what they "should" do.

Don't Try to Fix Them. You can't. Try to remember that grief is not something you can fix. It is a process.

Remember this: You don't have to understand or relate to a person's grief to help them heal. You only need to be empathetic, compassionate and allow them to process their feelings without judgment.

CHAPTER 5

Her Legacy

Losing my mom is the hardest, most painful thing I have ever experienced. In the first few months after her passing, I lost all motivation in my personal life and my professional life. The pain at times became unbearable. I was drowning in my grief. I stopped going to therapy and I wanted to give up on life. How was I supposed to go on without my mom?

I don't know the exact day that I had the epiphany. I do know that it was after one of my crying spells. I exited the closet with eyes swollen and full of tears. I looked in the mirror and saw my mom. For years I had noticed that the older I got, the more I looked like her. In that moment, I was reminded that everything that my mom was, is in me, too.

The tears began to fall as I started to think about how disappointed she must be at the person I had reduced myself to in her absence. I had become a shell of the woman she raised. In spite of my pain, I knew she deserved more. I made up my mind that I would do whatever I needed to do, to not only keep her memory alive, but to continue to make her proud and honor her in all that I do. In June 2020, ZDJ Enterprises and Red Ink Publishing were established in my mom's honor.

My mom's legacy lies in me. It lies in the unconditional love I have for my husband and children. It lies in the way I value my family and friends. It lies in my love for words and in the pursuit of my dreams. All of her years of sacrifices and tears were so that I could live the life she knew I was destined to live. She believed in me like only a mother could. There was nothing that she didn't believe that I could accomplish.

Everything that my mom instilled in me I carry in my spirit. If I am half as good a mom as Zerlin Dean Jones was to me, it would be the greatest accomplishment I will ever achieve.

During one of my last therapy sessions before I stopped going (Side note: I will be going back to therapy), my therapist asked me to consider writing a letter to my mom, to help me with the grieving process.I told her no and that I felt like writing a letter to her was saying goodbye… and I don't ever want to say goodbye.

As I close this chapter, I know that I am on a path to healing. I am learning to walk through grief in my own way. I have grown in ways that I never expected. On the days ahead, I still expect grief to be the same: ugly, unpredictable and messy. I still expect there to be days in which I am on the floor of my closet in the fetal position weeping.

But my mom's legacy will live on. It will live on through me and the lives of all who knew her. This continuation of her legacy is my letter to my mom.

The road ahead will be difficult. There will be days of tears and despair. There will be days of pain and heartache. There will be days that her absence seems unbearable. But there will also be days of joy and laughter. Allow yourself to enjoy the good days without guilt. Surround yourself with people who love you unconditionally and who can walk with you on this journey. I wish you love and healing, always.

May 10, 2020

Mother's Day. Three years...

Three years without my best friend to call. Three years without us laughing about the card and gift that she would receive in about 14-30 days. Three years without my Mama.

This morning I woke up the same way I went to sleep--in tears. I couldn't get myself together. My husband and the kids cooked breakfast. Saniya asked me if I wanted pancakes or french toast. I chose pancakes. Tre used my Keurig to make me some coffee and put it in my brand new coffee mug with elephants on it and they all served me breakfast in bed.

My husband came upstairs to check on me and brought with him my beautiful new elephant pen and blanket. I thanked him with about as much emotion as I could muster up. He knew I was appreciative but he also knew I was hurting. He asked me if I needed anything and then left me alone with my grief. He didn't want to, but he knew it was what I needed.

I stayed in bed and cried.

I told myself I wouldn't get on social media. I did. I shouldn't have. I saw the posts from fellow club members: the club of the motherless. It reminded me that I wasn't alone. And I saw all the posts of those who were enjoying time with their mothers (about as much as they could during this quarantine) and those sharing memories, pictures and videos. And it reminded me that I wouldn't be enjoying any of that. My mama was gone.

And as I continued to scroll and torture myself, I felt something that I never felt before...regret. All the pictures and videos all up and down my timeline of women enjoying time with their mothers, all the memories they made and captured. I didn't have any of that. The last two years of my mama's life and only a handful of pictures. Why didn't I take pictures or videos? She's gone forever. I wept.

I wept because I should have taken pictures, videos...something. I should have captured moments when she wasn't looking, or when she was asleep. Anything. I didn't because I knew how she felt about pictures, especially after she became sick. She didn't want pictures. I respected that. And I regret it.

My mama really did love pictures. But she loved taking them, not being in them. If you looked at pictures from birthday parties, family reunions, or trips, you would find her in those pictures with a smile as big as her personality. But that's about it. And honestly, I'm the same way. I take pictures when I have to, but I'd much rather not. I don't know how many times my husband and I have hosted or gone to an event, party, family gathering and come back home with absolutely no pictures of each other, just everybody else. That was my mama.

I stayed in bed most of the day in my regret and my grief. The door opened and I thought it was my husband. It was my son. "Mom, why are you still in bed?" I don't talk about my grief with my kids (it's something I'm working on) and my first thought was to say I wasn't feeling well. But I didn't. I told the truth. I told him I was sad and why I was sad. I asked him if he wanted me to get up . I was hoping he would say yes because I needed a reason outside of myself to drag my body out of that bed. He did want me to and so I got up, showered, did my hair and went downstairs.

My mama loved movies. Her favorites were comedies. I needed to laugh so I logged into BET+ and chose Back to the Goode Life. Without giving it away, there was a part in the movie when the dad talked to the daughter about the loss of her mom. He told her how the loss of her mom (his wife) affected him and about his grief. It resonated with me so much. It was what I needed to hear.

Then, I got back on social media and I saw a post from a person I admire, Ebony Stroder. In her post she said how amazing her Mother's Day was and even though she didn't get any pictures, the memories will be *in her heart forever. And it clicked. I may not have the pictures, but I have the memories. So many wonderful, cherished memories.*

I appreciate the fact that my husband and my kids allowed me to feel what I needed to feel and then get on with my day with them. It's what I needed. I don't know how long I will need it. But that's how it is right now. I didn't have to be fake. I didn't have to pretend, or wear my grief mask. This is my new normal. This is Mother's Day for me.

Raw. Real. Unapologetic.

A YEAR OF FIRSTS

The first year after the loss of your mom is full of grief triggers. They are the first reminders of your new normal. Here are a few tips to help on those days:

Her Birthday. Do an activity that she loved, volunteer at an organization that was important to her, or celebrate with family and friends. If you choose not to celebrate at all, know that it is okay.

On my mom's first birthday after her passing, family and friends in Mississippi visited her gravesite and did a balloon release. My oldest daughter and I drove to Wisconsin to participate in the Race to Cure Sarcoma Cancer 5K.

Your Birthday. Decide how you want to spend your day. If the first one is too difficult and you want to be alone, communicate that with your loved ones. Don't force it.

My birthday was one of my mom's favorite days to celebrate. I didn't want to acknowledge it or celebrate it after I lost her. But I also wanted to honor my mom, so I told my family and friends how I wanted to celebrate and what I needed on that day.

Her Deathiversary. This day is difficult because it brings up all of the raw emotions and reminds you of your loss all over again. You relive that day and it is painful. Plan ahead.

On the day of my mom's first deathiversary, my husband and I landed in Cancun for my friend's wedding. I took some time to myself to remember my mom. The second year, I didn't plan anything and spent the entire day in bed.

Her Favorite Holiday. Decorate with her favorite colors or incorporate something that she loved to do on that day. You can also consider starting a new tradition and honor her in some way.

My mom's favorite holiday was Christmas. This year we are considering starting a new family tradition of traveling to a different city to celebrate. My mom loved to travel.

Mother's Day. This is the most difficult day. Celebrate in your own way. Consider doing something she enjoyed. Limit social media. If you have kids, please set aside time for them to celebrate with you. If you are married or in a relationship, communicate with your spouse or significant other what you need. If you are single, talk to your family or close friends about your needs on that day.

My husband and kids serve me breakfast in bed and that's my way of celebrating with them. On Mother's Day 2020, I spent the rest of the day watching movies that my mom loved.

A LETTER OF LOVE

Date _____

Dear _____,

_____

_____

_____

_____

_____

_____

_____

_____

_____

_____

_____

_____

_____

_____

_____

_____

_____

F*CK CANCER

_____

_____

_____

_____

_____

_____

_____

_____

_____

_____

_____

_____

_____

_____

_____

_____

_____

_____

_____

_____

_____

_____

_____

_____

_____

F*CK CANCER

ACKNOWLEDGEMENTS

First and foremost, I have to thank God for the strength to put these words on these pages. He gave me the instructions to write this book months before my mom passed away. Almost three years later and it is finished. Delay does not mean denial.

To my loving and amazing husband, Sherwin - I don't know where to start. I could not have written this book without your unconditional love and support. You have been there for me in ways I didn't even know I needed. You love me past my pain. You were the apple of my mom's eye. Anyone who knew her knew how she felt about her son-in-law. Thank you for loving her, for making sure that I could be there for her throughout her illness, and for being my rock in her absence. It would take a dozen lifetimes to show you how much I love you.

To my kids, Kyndal, Saniya, and Tre - The love your Maw Maw had for you is unrivaled. It could not be put into words. You were her pride and joy. I hope that when you look at me, you see her. I pray that you will always keep her love and memory close to your hearts. And I pray that I am able to be the mother to you that she was to me.

To my NaNa - You are the epitome of strength. I thank God for sustaining you and keeping you through the tremendous loss that you have experienced. Within the last six years, you have lost your husband and two daughters, yet your faith in God was steadfast and unwavering. I love you with all my heart and soul. Mama left me in excellent hands.

Sadly, my NaNa never got a chance to read these words. On September 11, 2020, just six days after I announced the pre-order for this book, my NaNa, Alma B. Jones, passed away at 86.

To my Aunt Tammie and Uncle Mike - Thank you so much for always being there for me no matter what. I have always been able to depend on you, and for that I am grateful. I love you both.

To Uncee - You are the best big brother Mama could have ever been blessed with. I love you and I hope you always remember how much Mama loved you, too.

To my cousin, April - We are taking this walk together. I miss OT so much. We both have suffered a great loss and I'm thankful that we can support one another. I love you to the moon and back.

To my cousin Mikey (sorry, but you will never outgrow that nickname) - Your encouragement, wisdom, and transparency have gotten me through some extremely tough days. Mama was so proud of you. I love you to the moon and back.

To my cousin Derrick - I can always count on you to make me laugh. Thank you for keeping the light in my life and always brightening my day. I love you so much.

To my cousins, Mikailah, Mikiyah, and Miyah - I wish Mama was here to see the young women, and young lady, that you all have grown to be. I love you all and can't wait to see what's in store for you.

To my Uncle Scott - You helped my OT take care of Mama throughout her entire sickness. You kept her laughing with your amazing sense of humor. Thank you for all of your sacrifices.

To my girls, Brandie, Cybrina, Angelia, Ariane, Ashley, and Lakesia - You have been there for me through it all. You have pushed me, guided me, prayed for me and encouraged me. I could not have written this book without your support. I love you with all my heart.

To Brenessa - You and Mama were more like sisters than cousins. I can't thank you enough for the important role you played in her life. Thank you for everything you did for NaNa. Nothing has gone unnoticed.

To Pauline, Regina, Virlee, and Priscilla - Thank you for carrying the torch for Mama and helping to make sure that NaNa was taken care of. I love and appreciate you all.

To my Godmommy Annette - You were Mama's best friend. Thank you for loving her and being there for her. Thank you for always thinking about me and checking on me. You are loved.

To Pastor Brown and The New Zion Hill Baptist Church family - Thank you for your unconditional love and for continuing to honor Mama for her many years of service. NZHBC will always be my church home.

To my amazing team - You guys are the absolute best! I could not think of a more phenomenal group of women that I would have wanted to share this part of my journey with. I appreciate you all so much.

To anyone I may have missed - please forgive me and know that I appreciate you. Charge it to my head and not my heart.

And last but definitely not least, to my readers - Thank you from the bottom of my heart. Thank you for reading. I pray that this book helps you on your path to healing, just as it did mine.

ABOUT THE AUTHOR

K. Danielle is a poet, blogger, and children's book author from Mississippi whose love for reading and writing was nurtured by her mom, Zerlin Dean Jones. For K. Danielle, pursuing her career as an author is her contribution to her mom's legacy as it was her mom's dream that she become a successful author. In July 2020, she launched her second publishing company, Red Ink Publishing, in honor of her mom.

After losing her mom to cancer in 2017, K. Danielle was led to pen this book to help others cope with the tremendous loss of their mothers, as well as face her own battle with grief. It is her hope to comfort others by sharing her own experience of heartbreak.

K. Danielle began her writing career with the publication of Pieces of My Reflection written under the pen name JustasPoetic in 2015. It is a collection of poems that span ten years. Shortly after, she founded Peppermint Publishing and is diligently working on a series of books for young readers ages 4-9 about characters inspired by her children.

She resides in Indianapolis, IN with her husband, Sherwin, and her three children, Kyndal, Saniya, and Tre. In addition to writing, K. Danielle also provides virtual bookkeeping services to small businesses and non-profit organizations.

For more information, visit www.kdanielle.com.

FIVE WAYS TO SUPPORT AN AUTHOR

1. Leave a review on Amazon.
   Go to www.amazon.com.
   Search for F*ck Cancer, K. Danielle.
   Scroll down, and click "Write a customer review."

2. Follow me on social media.
   Facebook: The K. Danielle
   Instagram: @the_kdanielle
   Twitter: @the_kdanielle

3. Tell a friend about me.

4. Subscribe to my email list.
   www.thekdanielle.com

5. Share my book on social media.